When God
SHOWS UP

Essays on Revival

DAVID BUTTS
Foreword by Sammy Tippit

PRAYERSHOP
PUBLISHING

Terre Haute, Indiana

PrayerShop Publishing is the publishing arm of Harvest Prayer Ministries and the Church Prayer Leaders Network. Harvest Prayer Ministries exists to transform lives through teaching prayer. Its online prayer store, www.prayershop.org, has more than 600 prayer resources available for purchase.

ISBN: 978-1-935012-32-0

1 2 3 4 5 | 2017 2016 2015 2014 2013

TABLE OF CONTENTS

FOREWORD

We live in peculiar times. It's a period of history when there's been much discussion about the fires of revival, but hardly any embers are left to be seen; much talk about desperation, but few who are hungry and thirsty for God's presence; and a church with a history of embracing light, but dances with darkness. Christians seem to have more confidence in the power of political parties to change the nation than we have in the church to transform our culture. We've trusted in voting at the ballot box rather than praying.

A few years ago, I was keynote speaker on a statewide conference on spiritual awakening. One of the other speakers was the late Dr. Roy Fish, one of the great scholars on the 1857 revival that began in the business district of New York City. A participant in the meetings asked Dr. Fish, "Do you see any hope for revival in this generation?"

His response surprised everyone. "I see only one hope," he emphatically stated. "That hope is that we've become hopeless. It's when we're hopeless that God stirs in the hearts of His people to pray for revival."

With so much talk about spiritual awakening and very little of its reality, the rivers of revival have been muddied in the eyes of many believers. We've lost sight of the beauty and splendor of living in His manifest presence. It's in times like these that God burns a passionate cry for revival into the hearts of His servants–those with a heart to know Him intimately. He provides us with a clear word from His Word.

Dave Butts gives us this kind of uncompromising appeal in these essays. He presents us with a clarion call for revival in this generation. It's not rooted in the sensationalism of a circus styled revival or in the subjectivism of an intellectual analysis of spiritual awakening. It's birthed and developed in the Scriptures.

God has allowed me to witness this kind of outpouring of His Spirit on several occasions. The first time was in Monroe, Louisiana in 1970. It began with a praying pastor who was desperate to see God work in the hearts of the young people who had left his church. After months of praying, God not only shook his church but an entire city. The evening news and front page of the local paper carried major stories about the revival. Young people were set ablaze for Christ.

The next time was in East Germany in 1973, during the days of communism. A pastor and a layman desperately cried to God because an entire generation of youth left the church due to severe persecution of the communists. The two men prayed for more than a year for revival. Thousands of youth turned to Christ, and huge cathedrals were packed with young people seeking God.

Perhaps the greatest move of God's Spirit that I've witnessed was the revival that swept through Romania in the late 1980s. The darker the days became, the more fervently the Christians prayed. In one divine moment, everything changed. A revolution erupted in the nation. Hundreds of thousands who had been brainwashed with scientific atheism shouted in the streets, "Existe Dumnezeu! Existe Dumnezeu! (There is a God! There is a God!) How did they know? God visited the nation.

—Sammy Tippit

INTRODUCTION

Christians around the world are praying for revival. What exactly is meant by "revival"? Some think in terms of great meetings or tremendous evangelistic outreach. Others think more in terms of Christians who are encouraged and brought to a new level of commitment in their faith. Certainly Christians should be praying for revival, but what is it we are praying for and about?

Though many have given good definitions of revival, I still like this simple little description: Revival happens when God shows up for church. In a real sense, the Lord is always present when His people gather in His Name. But all too often His presence goes unnoticed. This definition recognizes that when the people of God become aware of the presence of the Lord, everything changes. Our worship services, our family lives, our evangelistic efforts, and our individual devotional lives will all be different when God shows up for church.

The Bible teaches us the amazing fact that God has come to dwell in us through His Holy Spirit. The Old Testament name given to the Messiah was Emmanuel . . . God with us. Colossians 1:27 teaches us the mystery of God: "Christ in [us], the hope of glory." Jesus said, "If anyone loves me, he will obey my teaching. My Father will love him, and we will come to him and make our home with him" (John 14:23). The Lord also made it clear that when two or more are gathered together, He will be there in our midst.

Much as the temple or the tabernacle in the Old Testament was a place where the presence of God was manifest on earth, the gathered church today has become a place where His presence is known. Our theology is clear on that fact. Unfortunately, our experience normally fails to match our theology. Most churches meet for worship, teaching, and fellowship and leave again without truly being aware of God in their midst.

Praying for revival is praying for the people of God to have open eyes. Lord, help us to see Jesus! Open the eyes of our hearts that we might know You and become aware of Your presence here in our lives.

The experience of Israel under the leadership of Moses is a great example for the church today as we cry out to God for revival. My friend Terry Teykl has written a powerful book entitled *The Presence Based Church*. He describes their experience:

As a result of their unique relationship with God, the Israelites became the original Presence based people. Under the leadership of Moses, and at God's bidding, they made the Presence the axis of their lives.

The Ark of the Covenant was always located in the tabernacle at the very center of the camp. The 12 tribes were divided into four groups and stationed symmetrically around the Presence: three to the north, three to the south, three to the east, and three to the west. By day they saw the cloud that hung over the tent, and by night they would lie in the entrance to their own tents and watch the fire. As long as the Presence stayed, they stayed. But when the Presence moved, they followed. They were Presence led and Presence drawn. (p. 89)

In Exodus 33, verses 13–17, there is a fascinating conversation between the Lord and Moses concerning His presence when Moses asks to learn God's ways.

> The LORD replied, "My Presence will go with you, and I will give you rest."
>
> Then Moses said to him, "If your Presence does not go with us, do not send us up from here. How will anyone know that you are pleased with me and with your people unless you go with us? What else will distinguish me and your people from all the other people on the face of the earth?"
>
> And the LORD said to Moses, "I will do the very thing you have asked, because I am pleased with you and I know you by name."

Moses understood how critical it was for Israel to stay with the presence of God. When the church today grabs hold of that fact, we will see revival. When the church, like Moses, commits to going only where the Lord leads, then we will be making progress. It is time for us to cry out for the Lord to make us aware of His presence.

Teykl offers great insight as to the effects of the manifest presence of God:

> Where His Presence is being manifested, God's glory is evident. When the Presence fell on the Mercy Seat of the Ark, His glory filled the tabernacle to such an extent that

no one could go near. His Presence was noticeable. Think about it. If God were to manifest His Presence in your church, shouldn't it be just as noticeable as it was in the tabernacle? Is not God that same God that descended in the Holy Place and rested among His chosen people in fire and cloud? Is He not the same God who, from the Mercy Seat, displayed His power and authority, guided and governed the Israelites, gave them victory over their enemies, demonstrated His favor and love, established His uniqueness and offered atonement for sin?

Where God's Presence is being manifested today, the same results are evident. Humility and uncommon zeal characterize people of the Presence because they have seen His power and know of His authority in the earth. Where the Presence is, wisdom and peace prevail through His guidance. Pathways become clear and sound decisions are made. In the Presence, people gain victory over habits or emotions that have held them captive for years. Relationships are healed, lives are transformed, joy is evident and the powers of darkness are forced to retreat. In the Presence, many call on the name of Jesus and are saved in response to the wave of supernatural love and grace that penetrates their spirits. (p. 201)

Does that sound a bit like revival to you? It does to me. I'm praying for an increased hunger for His presence in my life, my family, and my church. As God answers that prayer, we will begin to see an increased awareness of the activity of the Lord in the midst of His people. Join me in praying for God to "show up for church."

PRAYING FOR REVIVAL

Christians around the world are praying for revival. What does revival look like, how does it come about, and how do we pray for it? Do we have good reason to expect it? Is revival something God wants to do for His people today? To answer these questions, we need to understand that God has always worked in the area of revival with His people. From the earliest days of Israel on through the history of the church, God's method of dealing with His people has been to grant periodic times of special blessing in which His presence is made manifest and His people are drawn back to Him. The result of that is a changed society.

Revivals in History

Perhaps the clearest view of revival can be seen by looking back at Israel in the Old Testament. Historians tell us that there are seven major revivals in the Old Testament. I would suggest that if you take away the word "major" there are somewhere between fifteen and sixteen revivals. These are clear, distinct times in which the people of God were restored to a time of religious excitement, enthusiasm, and commitment with a resultant change in society.

You typically see something like this: Israel, as a people, called by God to make a difference . . . called to be a light to the Gentiles. You see the people under a leader, such as Moses or David, living a life that causes them to be set apart from the people around them. They are worshiping God, they're holding on to His Word, and they are doing what God wants them to do. Then, typically, after a generation or so when the leader has died, you see Israel begin to slide. You begin to see them move farther and farther away from obedience to the Word of God. They begin to accept idolatry from the tribes around them. Pagan practices come in, with acts of immorality and all the problems associated with that. And eventually times of war and even slavery come about.

Typically at this point of decline, there arises a remnant of people who begin to pray. They begin to cry out to God asking the Lord to save them. Then, in His own timing, God sends a leader and there comes a time of revival when the people begin to throw off their idolatry and paganism and to restore, once again, the true worship of Jehovah. They begin again to hold on to the Word of God. The nation experiences a time of prosperity, spiritual excitement, and religious significance that lasts about a generation. Then you see the cycle begin again. Over and over again, throughout the Old Testament, you have revival and decline, revival and decline.

As you move into the New Testament, you see a group of people who were born in a time of revival. But we know historically that it did not last. Through the history of the church, you once again see the same pattern of revival and decline. Revival seems to be the way God deals with His people when they grow spiritually cold. Down through the years, many countries have experienced periodic times of revival. Within the United States, we have experienced three times of national revival, known as the Great Awakenings. During these times, God moved and changed the course of our nation. Many of us believe that God is getting ready to do it again in our day, in our age.

Revival Defined for Today

What is this thing called revival? I believe that revival is the church waking up to the presence of Jesus in her midst. It is nothing more and nothing less than you and I beginning to experience what we already know theologically and intellectually. You believe that Jesus is with you. Why? Because He said He would be. You don't necessarily believe it because you feel Him, but just because Jesus said it. He said that where two or three are gathered together, there He is in our midst. You also have to believe Colossians 1:27: "Christ in you, the hope of glory."

We believe that Jesus is present when we gather as the church. But we don't act that way. That is not the way things happen on Sunday. You know why I know your church needs revival? The reason I know your church needs revival is because when church services ended last Sunday, you went home. What would happen if Jesus was there? Let's just suppose Jesus was there. Would you be looking at your watch? Would you be eager to leave? One of the characteristics of the great revivals was extended times of worship. They never wanted to end the service! Now obviously people had to leave, they had to take care of physical things, and they had jobs that they had to go to. But as soon as they were done, they were back, because that was where God was. They wanted to be in on the action. They wanted to be where God was. They wanted to experience His presence.

I suggest to you that revival is not strange or mystical. It is simply the church waking up to the presence of Christ in her midst. It is almost as though God reaches out and slaps us, and we wake up and realize God is there. That is what revival is. It is God shaking us. It is God waking us up. And we recognize that Jesus really is here.

We are desperate for that in our nation today. I am not in any way a critic of the church. The more I travel, the more I fall in love with the church of Jesus Christ. I am seeing so many wonderful things happen. Christians are doing wonderful things in the name of Jesus, acts of love, mercy, and self-sacrifice. It is amazing what is happening today and has been happening for years. We are doing all we know to do. But it isn't working.

Revival versus Programs or Activities

Most churches have all kinds of activities. They've tried all kinds of programs. They've given and done everything they know how to do to get the church going and to impact society. But in all that has happened in the last fifty years in the U.S. church, are we a more moral and ethical nation because of what we have been doing as a church? Regardless of the tremendous acts of sacrifice, service, and ministry in the last fifty years in the church, it is apparent that the church is going one way and our nation is moving the opposite way as fast as it can.

In a real sense, we are at this wonderful point of despair. We are at a wonderful point of hopelessness in which the church is beginning to recognize that we have been doing everything we know how to do and it is not working. This is the time for revival. It is time to humble ourselves before God in prayer and ask Him to make Himself known in the midst of His people so that our nation can be saved and our world impacted for Christ.

Preparation before Revival

How does revival come about? Any student of revival will tell you that there has never been a revival without a movement of prayer. God always calls His people to prayer in anticipation of revival. I ask you today to get serious about praying for revival. We need to shift our prayer focus to the issues that are close to God's heart; we need to pray especially that His people, His church, would wake up and discover the presence of Jesus in our midst.

When that happens, our lives become different. When Jesus is there, suddenly things that we accepted before are no longer acceptable. Some of the things that go on in our church and in our society are changed because the Lord is present. That is why in those great revivals in the past, there was a bit of emotionalism. Suddenly, they came into a church service and there was Jesus. Now they did not see Him in the flesh, but there was a powerful sense of the presence of Jesus. What do you suppose happens if you come into a church service during a revival and there is a strong sense of the presence of Jesus and you've been sinning all week? When you come into the presence of the awesome holiness of God, suddenly there is weeping, crying out, and sometimes even falling down before God in repentance.

Heaven-sent revival is our only hope. We don't have answers. We don't know what to do. We don't have any programs in our churches that are changing whole communities and our society. It's just not happening. What we need is God.

How do you pray for revival? Psalm 85:1–6 is a good place

to begin: "You showed favor to your land, O LORD; you restored the fortunes of Jacob. You forgave the iniquity of your people and covered all their sins. *Selah.* You set aside all your wrath and turned from your fierce anger. Restore us again, O God our Savior, and put away your displeasure toward us. Will you be angry with us forever? Will you prolong your anger through all generations? Will you not revive us again, that your people may rejoice in you?"

Based on that passage, we will pray, "Lord, revive us again. Do it again in our day." We will come before God saying, "Lord, this is what You have done, and this is what we want You to do in our life and in our nation."

THE REFRESHING RAIN OF THE LORD'S PRESENCE

"*L*et us acknowledge the LORD; let us press on to acknowledge him. As surely as the sun rises, he will appear; he will come to us like the winter rains, like the spring rains that water the earth" (Hosea 6:3).

"Sow for yourselves righteousness, reap the fruit of unfailing love, and break up your unplowed ground; for it is time to seek the LORD, until he comes and showers righteousness on you" (Hosea 10:12).

What is the rain we so long for and need? Ultimately, it is the Lord's presence. Jesus Himself spoke of the living water that we would need in our lives. The Scripture speaks of "times of refreshing" (Acts 3:19). Such a time is not so much an experience as it is a Person—a waking up to the presence of Christ in our lives.

Whether we are asking for ourselves, our church, or our nation, Hosea 10:12 gives us what we need to do to end drought and prepare for rain. Let's examine it phrase by phrase:

Sow Righteousness

"Sow for yourselves righteousness." Both Old and New Testaments teach us the spiritual principles that you reap what you sow. If you plant wheat, you will not harvest corn. If you plant immorality, you will harvest immorality. Much of the world has been sowing greed, pleasure, immorality, and self-centeredness—and we are reaping the results of that. Unfortunately, it is all too easy for the church to join with society in reaping the same damaging seed. God's Word says to sow righteousness; we need to sow right things. We must speak right things, watch right things, read right things, and do right things. The Bible becomes the means for us to see what those right things are. God's Word gives us a standard for righteousness. Righteousness is not what *seems* right to a person, but what *is* right to God.

Reap Love

"Reap the fruit of unfailing love." When righteousness has been sown, we will begin to harvest the fruit of unfailing love. God loves everyone, but the fruit, the benefits of that love, come to those who are moving to establish God's righteousness as the standard for their lives. There are many unclaimed blessings. One of the most neglected is the fruit of unfailing love. It only comes to those who have sown righteousness in their lives.

Plow the Ground

"Break up your unplowed ground." Unplowed ground has a hard time receiving rain. Sun-scorched, baked earth forms a hard crust, and when rain comes, it simply runs off rather than soaking in and making a difference. Unplowed ground is a picture of the unrepentant life. The rain of God's righteousness will not soak in and change a life that is hard and unrepentant. So the command here is "Repent! Change! Go a different direction!" That is always God's call to those seeking revival. Today, so many seeking revival, the rain from heaven, seem to want just good feelings or nice meetings. The good things of revival, however, come only after times of tears and repentance. God's command is to break up the hard, unplowed ground of your lives so you will then be ready for the rain of revival.

Seek the Lord

"It is time to seek the Lord." Those in periods of spiritual dryness often go looking for answers in many places. But God's Word directs us to the only place where we can experience renewal: the rain of heaven. And that means we must seek the Lord.

Hosea 10:12 gives great hope to us today. When we have broken up the unplowed ground in repentance and begin to seek the Lord with all our heart, then the promise comes. It is the Lord Himself Who comes in response to a repentant, seeking heart. He comes ready to shower His righteousness upon us. Jesus Himself walks in the midst of His people, receiving our worship and showering upon us the blessings of His presence.

A BURDEN FOR REVIVAL

evival comes to those who are desperate for it. Many people today are talking about spiritual awakening and even beginning to pray about it. But have we allowed God to place within us the burden necessary to pray desperately for God to show up in our midst? Are we willing to pray the price to see God move in a powerful way in the church today? As I continue to learn how to move my prayers into alignment with God's will, praying Scripture has become increasingly important. As I pray God's Word, I find myself praying in ways I would never have thought of praying. So it is as we begin to place ourselves before the Lord in asking for a burden for revival. I have been greatly impacted by the prayer of the psalmist in Psalm 79.

This is a powerful prayer for revival. It was prayed from a broken heart that saw the people of God under attack and the promises of God unfulfilled. Here it is:

1. "God, the nations have invaded your inheritance; they have defiled your holy temple, they have reduced Jerusalem to rubble."
2. "They have given the dead bodies of your servants as

food to the birds of the air, the flesh of your saints to the beasts of the earth."

3. "They have poured out blood like water all around Jerusalem, and there is no one to bury the dead."

4. "We are objects of reproach to our neighbors, of scorn and derision to those around us."

5. "How long, O LORD? Will you be angry forever? How long will your jealousy burn like fire?"

6. "Pour out your wrath on the nations that do not acknowledge you, on the kingdoms that do not call on your name;"

7. "for they have devoured Jacob and destroyed his homeland."

8. "Do not hold against us the sins of the fathers; may your mercy come quickly to meet us, for we are in desperate need."

9. "Help us, O God our Savior, for the glory of your name; deliver us and forgive our sins for your name's sake."

10. "Why should the nations say, 'Where is their God?' Before our eyes, make known among the nations that you avenge the outpoured blood of your servants."

11. "May the groans of the prisoners come before you; by the strength of your arm preserve those condemned to die."

12. "Pay back into the laps of our neighbors seven times the reproach they have hurled at you, O Lord."

13. "Then we your people, the sheep of your pasture, will praise you forever; from generation to generation we will recount your praise."

Praying through Psalm 79 is a great way to develop a biblical burden for revival. The text breaks down into a great outline for passionate prayer:

Step 1: Recognizing your current situation is a critical place to begin. The people of Israel were oppressed . . . under attack by their enemies. They finally got to a place of desperation—"for we are in desperate need" (v. 8). Until the church today arrives at that place of desperation, we will never develop a burden for revival.

Step 2: Getting serious about the glory of God is the next step. Pagans were disparaging God because of the sorry situation of the Israelites. "Where is their God?" the ungodly asked. The fact that the world would ask such a question should bring great grief to God's people. In a very real sense, this is exactly what the world is saying of the church today: "Where is your God?"

Step 3: Recognizing your current situation and passion for God's glory will lead you to petition. At this point, we find Israel praying for mercy, deliverance, and forgiveness. It is a personal sort of prayer that focuses on the needs of the people of God for restoration into the favor of God.

Step 4: In the next step, we see the psalmist asking God to come into the situation. In a real sense, the psalmist prays, "God, You answer the accusations of the enemy. By Your actions, Lord, pay back the reproach that the world has heaped upon You through the sad condition of Your people."

Step 5: Praising and worshiping God is the result of such prayer. As we see God work, we naturally praise and worship Him. Even before full-blown revival arrives, worship erupts from the people of God. And along with that is the commitment to pass it on to the next generation.

Praying such a prayer for revival is not a guarantee of revival. It is merely preparing the ground of the human heart for a fresh work of God. Praying with passion for revival begins to create a burden for revival among the Lord's people. And into such a prepared state, the Lord has often poured His rain from heaven.

Martyn Lloyd-Jones speaks of this preparatory work of prayer in his book *Revival*:

> Our essential trouble is that we are content with a very superficial and preliminary knowledge of God, His being, His cause. . . . [We] spend our lives in busy activism . . . instead of realizing our own failure, (that) we are not attracting anybody to Christ and that they probably see nothing in us that makes them desire to come to Him.
>
> The inevitable and constant preliminary to revival has always been in a thirst for God, a thirst, a living thirst for a knowledge of the living God and a longing and a burning desire to see Him acting, manifesting Himself and His power, rising and scattering His enemies. . . . [The] thirst for God and the longing for the exhibition of His glory are the essential preliminaries to revival. (pp. 90–91)

May our prayers for revival develop a great thirst for God, not only in our own lives but in the lives of those around us.

PERSONAL REVIVAL

*L*ike a mighty wave rolling across the church around the world comes the cry from millions of believers: "Oh God, send a revival!" Like no time in recent history, the church is becoming aware of its own desperate condition and the even more critical needs of our culture. It is reassuring to know that for once, the church is not looking to another program or strategy to try to change the world. We're recognizing that it is going to take heaven-sent revival. Taking our cue from past revivals, Christians are praying for God to move in significant new ways in the church. It is these praying Christians who will experience in their own lives the first fruits of revival.

What is it we are praying for when we ask God to send revival? To fully answer that question would require a book, and even then perhaps it would be inadequate. Christian scholars are continuously debating the nature of revival. But, praise God, though we disagree on its nature, there is near unanimity on our desperate need for it. Some of my favorite short definitions of revival are as follows:

- "[A] movement of the Holy Spirit bringing about a revival of New Testament Christianity in the church of

Christ and its related community." —J. Edwin Orr
- "Revival is a community saturated with God." —Duncan Campbell
- "Revival is the Church falling in love with Jesus all over again." —Vance Havner

Perhaps the definition that best fits my own understanding is from Stephen Olford, who says, "Revival is ultimately Christ Himself, seen, felt, heard, living, active, moving in and through His Body on earth." True revival is not man-centered but Christ-centered. It is not about a type of music or special experience, but a fresh revelation of Christ in the midst of His people—people often grown sleepy or slow moving and desperately in need of a fresh awakening touch from their Savior.

Much has been written on what happens when revival touches a church, community, or nation. Foundational to each of those spheres of revival is a fresh touch from Christ upon an individual. J. Edwin Orr speaks of those different spheres this way: "Such an awakening may change in a significant way an individual; or it may affect a larger group of believers; or it may move a congregation or the churches in the city or district, or the body of believers throughout a country or continent; or indeed, the larger body of believers throughout the world."

What would it mean for an individual to experience revival? It is an important question for us to consider. Though we may long for and pray for revival for the whole church, we certainly want to make sure that revival could come to an individual apart from the corporate aspect. Dare we begin to ask God for revival in our own lives?

I believe there is a clear correlation between what happens when a church experiences revival and when an individual Christian experiences revival. The heart of revival is when Christ shows up for church. It is when we begin to experience what we already know is true biblically and theologically concerning the presence of Christ. One of the major tenets of our faith is that when believers in Jesus gather, He Himself is present in a very special way in their midst. Jesus said, "For where two or three come together in my name, there am I with them" (Matthew 18:20). We believe His words concerning His presence as we gather. Yet Sunday after Sunday in the majority of our churches, we go through the motions without a real awareness of Jesus actually being there with us. In revival, there is an awakening to His presence. Biblical truths that had perhaps grown stale are suddenly infused with new life. The love and life of Jesus are lived out in fresh new ways as the church gathers.

This same experience ought to mark the life of the individual Christian as we begin to experience revival personally. Colossians 1:27 says, "Christ in us, the hope of glory." Is there a more astonishing verse in Scripture—that the Son of God has actually come to take up residence within the individual Christian? Yet we often view such a verse as dry biblical truth. It somehow fails to excite or thrill the soul. Even more telling, it fails to change the way we live.

What a difference it would make in our lives if we truly lived out the truth of Christ in us, the hope of glory; if we were walking daily with Jesus—aware of His presence, His love, His strength, and His direction. Rather than asking the question in abstract, "What would Jesus do?," we would often throughout each day directly ask our indwelling Lord, "Jesus, what are you doing?" What a revival of changed life, character, and witness we would see among believers.

The nineteenth century Quaker author Hannah Whitall Smith wrote about this:

> Dear friend, I make the glad announcement to thee that the Lord is in thy heart. Since the day of thy conversion He has been dwelling there, but thou hast lived on in ignorance of it. Every moment during all that time might have been passed in the sunshine of His sweet presence, and every step have been taken under His advice. But because thou knew it not, and did not look for Him there, thy life has been lonely and full of failure. But now that I make the announcement to thee, how wilt thou receive it? Art thou glad to have Him? Wilt thou throw wide open every door to welcome Him in? Wilt thou joyfully and thankfully give up the government of thy life into His hands? Wilt thou consult Him about everything, and let Him decide each step for thee, and mark out every path? Wilt thou invite Him into thy innermost chambers, and make Him the sharer in thy most hidden life? Wilt thou say "Yes" to all His longing for union with thee, and with a glad and eager abandonment hand thyself and all that concerns thee over into His hands? If thou wilt, then shall thy soul begin to know something of the joy of union with Christ.

On a practical level, how can we begin to walk in this intimate relationship with Jesus? Years ago, I heard Argentine evangelist Juan Carlos Ortiz say "to walk in the Spirit is to be continually conscious of Christ in you." One of the major goals of my life has been to narrow the gaps of unawareness. It is so easy to get caught up in the activities of daily life—even in service to Jesus—and forget the awesome fact of the indwelling Christ.

Scriptures are so clear that our lives are hidden with Christ, that we are seated with Christ, and that we are to follow Him. Paul would go so far as to say, "I no longer live, but Christ lives in me" (Galatians 2:20). True spiritual awakening begins on a personal basis as we live out daily the truth of God's Word, "Christ in us, the hope of glory!"

A PROPER REACTION TO PERSONAL SIN

As Christians pray for revival, most of us understand, at some level, that our own sin indicates the need for revival and that our sin may also be blocking the coming of revival. Looking to past revivals for guidance, it seems that without repentance, there may be no expectation of revival. Therefore, it becomes imperative that we learn how to deal with our own sin.

Dealing with personal sin is something that should be taught at an early stage in our Christian life. It is a reality that we must learn to wrestle with. The apostle John tells us, "If we claim to be without sin, we deceive ourselves" (1 John 1:8). How do Christians deal with personal sin in an intentional way so that we are not deceived? There appear to be two extremes that many believers struggle with. One extreme that seems prevalent in the church today is to ignore sin, or to distort its seriousness. We lose sight of the call to holiness and what it means to follow Jesus. The other extreme is to be afraid that every time you sin you've lost your salvation. There are those who live in such a state of fear that they can hardly function as Christians.

The biblical way to deal with personal sin is perhaps best found in Psalm 51. David wrote and prayed this psalm right after he had been exposed as an adulterer and murderer. We can learn the proper reaction to personal sin from David.

First, there must be an acknowledgement of sin. Until we accept the fact that there is sin in our lives, there can be no confession, forgiveness, or restoration. Confession is basically agreeing with God that what we have done is sin. In Psalm 51:4, David makes the important step of realizing that sin is an affront to God Himself: "Against you, you only, have I sinned and done what is evil in your sight." When we understand this fact, sorrow for our sin becomes real and leads to further steps.

As David begins to understand the depths of his sin, he expresses his desire for cleansing and forgiveness. In his eagerness to receive forgiveness, he uses a variety of terms: "have mercy," "blot out," "wash away," "cleanse." It all comes down to asking God for forgiveness. The promise of Scripture is that God *will* forgive. It is important for Christians to memorize and believe with all their hearts the truth of 1 John 1:9: "If we confess our sins, he is faithful and just and will forgive us our sins and purify us from all unrighteousness."

True repentance never stays merely at the stage of confessing sin and desiring forgiveness. It moves us beyond that to a desire for a pure heart. There comes a longing to stay out of sin . . . to walk in victory. It means crying out, "O God, don't let me do this again!" David prayed this way: "Create in me a pure heart, O God, and renew a steadfast spirit within me" (Psalm 51:10). In asking for a new heart, we realize the need for sanctification, the power not to sin.

In our Christian walk, we will sin. But our desires, because of Christ, have changed. In fact, we have come to hate sin, especially in ourselves. Our desire is now for purity and holiness. If that desire is not in you, then you've never fully dealt with sin in your life. All too many Christians short-circuit the process of repentance and stop before they get to this point. If you are actively engaged in sin, please ask the Lord for strength to confess it, repent of it, and renounce it once and for all!

What happens in us after we have gone through this process of confession and repentance? David's response to forgiveness was to experience a restoration of joy and praise. "Restore to me the joy of your salvation and grant me a willing spirit, to sustain me" (Psalm 51:12). "O Lord, open my lips, and my mouth will declare your praise" (Psalm 51:15). God's people are a worshiping people. They are a forgiven people who have something to shout about, and who have a reason for joy. Peter writes, "But you are a chosen people, a royal priesthood, a holy nation, a people belonging to God, that you may declare the praises of him who called you out of darkness into his wonderful light" (1 Peter 2:9). Praise is what forgiven people do!

David even goes beyond worship in his response to the forgiveness of God. He did not keep what God had done bottled up inside him. He had been forgiven, and he wanted the world to know it. He declared, "Then I will teach transgressors your ways, and sinners will turn back to you" (Psalm 51:13). If we are going to be effective in sharing the gospel, it's going to be because we really believe that God has done something tremendous in our lives and we want that to happen in others' lives, too.

How do you deal with sin in your life? God has provided the answer to your sins in the person of Jesus. He doesn't want a single one of us to walk around burdened by sin. Perhaps right now is the time to bring your sins to the only One who can deal with them. Church attendance won't cleanse you from sin. Ministry and acts of service won't take care of your sin. Only Jesus can do that. God is calling the church to repentance! Turn from sin! Agree with God about the sinfulness of your sin. Ask for forgiveness. Trust in the cleansing blood of Jesus to provide not only forgiveness, but also the power to avoid sin in the future. Begin today to sing the praises of the One who has washed you and made you clean forever.

"Repent, then, and turn to God, so that your sins may be wiped out, that times of refreshing may come from the Lord" (Acts 3:19).

A MODEL FOR REVIVAL PRAYING IN PSALM 74

*F*or many years now, the Lord has put the issue of revival praying upon my heart.

Initially, I must admit, my prayers were fairly generic: "O Lord, please revive us." As I have grown in my approach to prayer, I've learned more specific requests, especially in using the Word of God to help format and provide content for my prayers. Psalm 80 and Isaiah 63 and 64 have helped me to petition the Lord for revival with both variety and the power of Scripture behind my requests.

Recently, I have been praying through the Psalms again. I began to lift before the Lord the words of Psalm 74. To my delight, I found another "revival" prayer. My desire is that this psalm will provide fuel for the fire of intercession and petition in your life as you beseech God to once again bless us with His presence in revival.

As you pray through Psalm 74, please notice that below, before major sections, I share some comments to help you see the aspects of revival in each passage. I encourage you to move beyond Bible study, however, to passionately praying the heart of the psalmist.

The Realization of the Need for Revival

At the beginning of Psalm 74, we find the agonizing realization that God's presence is not near. In fact, because of sin, there has been a sense of rejection. As is typical in revival praying, there is a cry for God to remember His people and return to them:

> Why have you rejected us forever, O God? Why does your anger smolder against the sheep of your pasture? Remember the people you purchased of old, the tribe of your inheritance, whom you redeemed—Mount Zion, where you dwelt. Turn your steps toward these everlasting ruins, all this destruction the enemy has brought on the sanctuary. (Psalm 74:1–3)

The Result of God's Apparent Absence

As we continue reading, we see that when sin is accepted in the life of the people of God, the consequences begin to be felt. The enemies of God and His people begin to afflict the nation. Notice that the psalmist uses the phrase, "Your foes roared." This reminds us that our ultimate enemy is Satan, the one whom Peter tells us roams about as a roaring lion seeking whom he might devour (1 Peter 5:8).

> Your foes roared in the place where you met with us; they set up their standards as signs. They behaved like men wielding axes to cut through a thicket of trees. They smashed all the carved paneling with their axes and hatchets. They burned your sanctuary to the ground; they de-

filed the dwelling place of your Name. They said in their hearts, 'We will crush them completely!' They burned every place where God was worshiped in the land. We are given no miraculous signs; no prophets are left, and none of us knows how long this will be. (Psalm 74:4–9)

An Awareness of the God to Whom We Pray

An important lesson to learn in prayer is that ultimately we need to be concerned about God and His reputation and the extension of His kingdom and purposes. Revival really isn't about us having better meetings or being happy. It is about God's Name being exalted and more praise and honor given to Him on this planet. Notice that the psalmist asked God to go to work, because He is the one being reviled and mocked through the attacks on His people. Note also that this portion of the psalm then moves into a wonderful expression of recognizing God's power and ability to handle any attack. As we understand the awesome power of the One we are addressing in prayer, our faith will grow and we will begin to pray in a way that moves the hand of God.

How long will the enemy mock you, O God? Will the foe revile your name forever? Why do you hold back your hand, your right hand? Take it from the folds of your garment and destroy them!

But you, O God, are my king from of old; you bring salvation upon the earth. It was you who split open the sea by your power; you broke the heads of the monster in

the waters. It was you who crushed the heads of Levia-
than and gave him as food to the creatures of the desert.
It was you who opened up springs and streams; you dried
up the ever flowing rivers. The day is yours, and yours
also the night; you established the sun and moon. It was
you who set all the boundaries of the earth; you made
both summer and winter. (Psalm 74:10–17)

The Request for Revival

Once again, this prayer is focused upon the honor of God and the
integrity of His covenant with His people. The concern is for the
Lord and how He is perceived by the nations. The cry for God to
rise up and defend His cause will mean that Israel will once again
walk in right relationship to their God. When He prospers them,
they cry that God will be honored, not only by Israel, but also by
those nations in the area who see how He protects and prospers His
people when they obey Him.

Remember how the enemy has mocked You, O LORD,
how foolish people have reviled your name. Do not hand over
the life of your dove to wild beasts; do not forget the lives of
your afflicted people forever. Have regard for your covenant,
because haunts of violence fill the dark places of the land.
Do not let the oppressed retreat in disgrace; may the poor
and needy praise your name. Rise up, O God, and defend
your cause; remember how fools mock you all day long. Do
not ignore the clamor of your adversaries, the uproar of your
enemies, which rises continually. (Psalm 74:18–23)

Our Prayer

Here is a prayer to pray that embraces the principles of revival in Psalm 74 and makes them our own:

Father, like ancient Israel, we too live in a day in which Your Name is mocked. Many times this happens because of the shortcomings and sins of those of us who are followers of Your holy Son, Jesus. Lord, we confess our sins and the way we have lived our lives as Christians apart from complete dependence upon You. We repent of this shameful self-sufficiency and throw ourselves upon Your mercy.

Gracious God, our lifestyle has often led unbelievers to insult and attack Your very nature and character. We ask You, Lord, to rise up and defend Yourself. Would You awaken Your people to the reality of Your presence in our midst and in so doing transform our lives into the character of Christ that You desire to see in us? May Your life lived out in Your church begin to demonstrate to the world Your love, grace, mercy, and overwhelming power on behalf of Your saints. Would You allow the kingdom principles that govern heaven to begin to be made manifest on earth? We ask You to revive Your people so that we may rejoice in You and demonstrate in our lives the awesome, transforming power of Jesus Christ in His church. Amen.

KINGDOM-FOCUSED PRAYER
OR REVIVAL PRAYER

The following is edited from a workshop presentation given at the Heart-Cry for Revival Conference in April 2008 at Asheville, North Carolina, U.S.A.

The issue in churches today is not that we are not praying, because every church prays some. The problem is that rarely do we pray what I call kingdom-focused prayers. Most of our churches are praying self-focused, need-focused prayers—our needs, our families, and things right around us. We are supposed to pray for those things, but that is only one aspect for which we ought to be praying. We also should be praying every day for the completion of the task of world evangelization, for revival, for our governmental leaders, for the unsaved. Those are kingdom-focused prayers.

A Correct Concept of Revival

In many churches, it is necessary to move the people away from the common concept of revival as a week of meetings or something that we schedule. True revival is heaven-sent and is in God's hands. Having a correct concept of revival helps us know what we are praying toward. Good definitions of revival help people stay focused as they pray.

Here are several definitions of revival. Arthur Wallis wrote, "Revival is such a display of God's holiness and power that often human personalities are overshadowed and human programs abandoned. It is God breaking into the consciousness of men in majesty and glory." Earlier I mentioned Vance Havner's definition, "Revival is the Church falling in love with Jesus all over again," and Duncan Campbell's definition, "Revival is a community saturated with God." The South African revivalist Andrew Murray said, "A true revival means nothing less than a revolution, casting out a spirit of worldliness and selfishness and making God in His love triumph in the heart and life."

As I said before, my favorite definition is from Stephen Olford: "Revival is ultimately Christ Himself seen, felt, heard, living, active, moving in and through His body on earth." The whole idea of revival is a Christ awakening. The true church *believes* that Jesus is in their midst, but is somehow failing to *experience* it. There is a great divide between our intellectual, theological, and biblical belief and what we actually experience. Revival crosses that divide.

Without thoughtful definitions in mind, we find ourselves praying for revival amiss. In praying for revival, don't discount the time you spend at the beginning of a prayer meeting or even in your own personal prayer life on understanding what it is you are praying toward and what you are asking God to do. You might be asking for something you want that is not something He desires.

To understand revival prayer or kingdom-focused prayer, we must open God's Word and learn to pray Scripture. We want to learn to pray for what God desires to have happen. Before I go on, I want to say I prefer the term "revival praying" rather than "praying for revival." If I am praying *for* revival, I become revival focused sometimes rather than focused on Christ. I tend to get more interested in something that happens with meetings. For some people, this is a small distinction. For me, revival praying is the type of praying that prepares the ground, or prepares the way for revival. Sometimes we ask God for something for which we are not ready.

I like to think of revival praying in terms of preparing ourselves for the outpouring of the Holy Spirit. The Old Testament talks about plowing up hard or fallow ground, so that if the rain was to fall on it, then it would not just run off. If nothing has been done to the ground, it will not be prepared to receive anything from heaven.

I think the same thing has happened when we persist in praying to God, "Give us revival! Give us revival!" What happens will be short-lived if the ground has not been prepared, if we have not prepared ourselves for the Holy Sprit to be poured upon us and to stay and to make some significant changes in our lives.

The Necessity of Prayer

Prayer and revival seem tied together. As far as we have been able to tell, there has never been a revival without there first being a move of prayer. A. T. Pierson said, "From the day of Pentecost there has not been one spiritual awakening in any land which has not begun in a union of prayer, though only among two or three. No outward, upward movement has continued after such prayer meetings have declined." It is interesting that he would suggest that it is the prayer meeting that not only helps usher in revival but even sustains it. As we look at some revivals, there is that truth that after revival has come and the prayer meetings are left behind, we soon find a decline in that revival.

Charles Spurgeon wrote, "O men and brethren, what would this heart feel if I could but believe that there were some among you who would go home and pray for a revival, men whose faith is large enough and their love fiery enough to lead them from this moment to exercise unceasing intercessions that God would appear among us and do wondrous things here as in the times of former generations." What would happen if there were men and women who read this and closed the book and had almost continuous intercession that God would move in our midst?

Much has been written about revival prayer and why it is so necessary. Here is a selection:

- T. Pierson wrote, "Closet communion needs time for the revelation of God's presence. It is vain to say, 'I have too much work to do to find time.' You must find time or forfeit blessing. God knows how to save time for you, time that you sacredly keep for time with Him."
- J. Gordon wrote, "To arouse one man or woman to the tremendous power of prayer for others is worth more than the combined activity of a score of average Christians."
- McGregor wrote, "I would rather train twenty men to pray than a thousand to preach. A minister's highest mission should be to teach His people to pray."
- Leonard Ravenhill wrote, "The true man of God is heartsick, grieved at the worldliness of the Church, grieved at the toleration of sin in the Church, grieved at the prayerlessness in the Church. He is disturbed that

the corporate prayer of the Church no longer pulls down the strongholds of the devil."

- Andrew Bonar said, "We must continue in prayer if we are to get an outpouring of the Spirit. Christ says there are some things we shall not get unless we pray and fast. Yes, prayer and fasting. We must control the flesh and abstain from whatever hinders direct fellowship with God."

- John R. Mott said, "The missionary church is a praying church. The history of missions is the history of prayer. Everything vital to the success of the world's evangelization hinges on prayer. Are thousands of missionaries and tens of thousands of native workers needed? *Pray ye therefore the Lord of the harvest, that He would send forth laborers into His harvest*" (Luke 10:2).

- Samuel Chadwick wrote, "We give ourselves to prayer. We preach a Gospel that saves to the uttermost and witnesses to its power. We do not argue about worldliness; we witness. We do not discuss philosophy; we preach the Gospel. We do not speculate about the destiny of sinners; we pluck them as brands from the burning. We ask no man's patronage; we beg no man's money; we fear no man's frown. Let no man join us who's afraid. We want none but those who are saved, sanctified and aflame with the fire of the Holy Ghost."

- Robert Speer wrote, "The evangelization of the world in this generation depends first of all upon a revival of prayer. Deeper than the need for men, deeper far than the need for money, deeper down at the bottom of our spiritless life is the need for the forgotten secret of prevailing, worldwide prayer."

- John R. Mott also said, "Prayer alone will overcome the gigantic difficulties that confront the workers in every field."
- Pierson wrote, "The Word of God represents all the possibilities of God as at the disposal of true prayer."
- William Carey wrote, "Prayer—secret, fervent, believing prayer—lies at the root of all personal godliness."

One of the men whose writings have impacted me greatly is Paul Billheimer. He wrote, "Satan does not care how many people read about prayer, if only he can keep them from praying. When a church is truly convinced that prayer is where the action is, that prayer will so construct its corporate activities that the prayer program will have the highest priority."

To be the kind of place that Billheimer describes, something has to change at the level of the local church. We have to do things differently. We cannot use prayer any longer just to open and close meetings. If we are a house of prayer, it means that prayer has to be woven into the fabric of who we are as a congregation.

Matthew Henry said, "When God is about to give His people the expected good, He pours out a spirit of prayer and it is a good sign that He is coming toward them in mercy. Then when you see the expected end approaching, then you shall call upon Me. Note that promises are not given to supersede but to quicken and encourage prayer, and when deliverance is coming, we must go forth by prayer to meet it. When Daniel understood that the seventy years were near expiring, then he set his face with more fervency than ever to seek the Lord."

Hudson Taylor said, "Since the days of Pentecost has the whole Church ever put aside every other work and waited upon Him for ten days, that the Spirit's power might be manifested? We give too much attention to method and machinery and resources, and too little to the source of power."

George Whitefield wrote this in his journal: "Whole days and weeks have I spent prostrate on the ground in silent or vocal prayer."

I love history. I love to hear about Whitefield and Wesley and Jonathan Edwards. Most of us love to hear those stories, but most of us aren't willing to pay the price. These men prayed. Whole days and weeks were spent prostrate on the ground in prayer. Whitfield should not be known only for his great preaching. We should remember him for great praying as well. As we look at how we might be used by God in praying for revival through revival praying, I believe that above all we must learn to become men and women who take God's Word back to Him in prayer. To do otherwise is to pray ineffectively.

A Key to Effective Revival Praying

During my high school years, someone put a book on revival in my hands, and I began praying for revival. I spent more than a decade praying for revival, not knowing exactly what I was praying for and not doing much of what I would call revival praying. I simply prayed, "Lord, send revival!" Now I know that is a childish prayer. It is a beginning place, but it is just an introduction to more informed prayer. We've got to move beyond that to the kind of prayer that prepares the ground, prepares our hearts, and prepares the life of the church. Part of my hopefulness for a coming revival is because I am seeing the church increasingly grow in this area. Not whole churches but groups of people. Many times revival comes through small groups who are passionately praying and literally laying before God the promises that He has expressed are His desire for His people, learning to pray His heart.

A key to praying for revival, although it can be applied into any area of our lives, is that we must learn to pray the Word of God and allow it to format our prayers. Doing so helps us learn to pray not so much what is on our hearts but what is on God's heart. It gives us a vocabulary for prayer. We pray on a different level with much greater effectiveness when we take God's Word and come before Him and say, "Lord, You have said…. You have revealed Your heart on this matter. Will You fulfill Your Word in our day? Would You do what You have promised to do?" Do not pull things out of context and do what you want with it. Instead, be earnest in seeking God's heart, coming to the Word and saying, "Lord, what is it *You* want to happen?" In 1 John 5:14–15 we read: "If we ask anything according to his will, he hears us. And if we know that he hears us—whatever we ask—we know that we have what we asked of him."

I want to share with you some of the passages of Scripture that you can use, some "fuel for the fire." You may want to start reading your Bible again while wearing your "revival glasses." Look for a move of God in the midst of His people. Look for times when God had left His people because of their sin and disobedience and then difficulties arose and in desperation God's people began to cry out to Him. See how the Lord responded. Sometimes you will see things in a verse or two, and sometimes it will be in a whole chapter.

Bible scholars point to at least seven major revivals in the Old Testament. From my study, if you take away the word "major," I find fifteen or sixteen distinct times of decline and revival in the Old Testament. If you read from the perspective of church history, you can see how God's heart is inclined to draw His people back when they have moved away from Him and then cry out to Him. He responds to that cry. This gives us great expectation for our day.

The Picture of Revival in Psalm 80

Psalm 80 is a powerful picture of revival. "Hear us, O Shepherd of Israel, you who lead Joseph like a flock; you who sit enthroned between the cherubim, shine forth before Ephraim, Benjamin and Manasseh. Awaken your might; come and save us. *Restore us, O God; make your face shine upon us, that we may be saved*" (vv. 1–3). [emphasis added]

"O Lord God Almighty, how long will your anger smolder against the prayers of your people?" At what kind of prayers is God angry? "You have fed them with the bread of tears; you have made them drink tears by the bowlful. You have made us a source of contention to our neighbors, and our enemies mock us." Then here again is the cry, *"Restore us, O God Almighty; make your face shine upon us, that we may be saved"* (vv. 4–7). [emphasis added]

Continuing on we read: "You brought a vine out of Egypt; you drove out the nations and planted it. You cleared the ground for it, and it took root and filled the land. The mountains were covered with its shade, the mighty cedars with its branches. It sent out its boughs to the Sea, its shoots as far as the River. Why have you broken down its walls so that all who pass by pick its grapes? Boars from the forest ravage it and the creatures of the field feed on it. Return to us, O God Almighty! Look down from heaven and see! Watch over this vine, the root your right hand has planted, the son you have raised up for yourself. Your vine is cut down, it is burned with fire; at your rebuke your people perish. Let your hand rest on the man at your right hand, the son of man you have raised up for yourself. Then we will not turn away from you; revive us, and we will call on your name. *Restore us, O Lord God Almighty; make your face shine upon us, that we may be saved"* (vv. 8–19). [emphasis added]

Can you imagine your congregation coming together and praying that prayer? Let the congregation begin to pray that passage, which is repeated until it becomes a passionate cry of the people of God: "Restore us, O Lord God Almighty; make Your face shine upon us, that we may be saved!" The church has to begin to cry out like this.

The Revival in Psalm 74

The Psalms are filled with prayers of revival. One of my favorites is Psalm 74, which I explained earlier is a useful model for revival.

Read Psalm 74 and let it be the cry of your heart. Verse 1 reads: "Why have you rejected us forever, O God? Why does your anger smolder against the sheep of your pasture?" Do you ever feel like that? Do you ever feel left to yourself? There is a story of the Chinese brother, the house church leader, who was arrested again and again and beaten over and over again and finally was expelled from China. He came to the United States and spent a year traveling to churches here. Everyone treated him royally, but finally the door opened up for him to try to get back into China. Before he left he met with a number of American church leaders, and they asked him to honestly tell them his opinion of the church in the United States. He thought carefully and then he said, "It is amazing to me how much you have been able to accomplish without God." Oh, might the church in America beware of being an abomination to God because she is not depending on Him!

As we read on in Psalm 74, we find an important principle of revival praying. There is a passion for the honor of God. It is not so much, "God, we are in trouble! Help us!" That is part of it, but there is also revival praying that says, "O God, rise up and defend Your Name, Your cause. Lord, You are the One being mocked. We are concerned about *Your* reputation, *Your* glory, *Your* Name." One of the effective ways of praying for revival is this concern about God and about how people are reproaching God. Being concerned about His honor and His glory is a principle found in a number of psalms.

Here are several other Scriptures helpful for revival praying: Psalm 85; Hosea 10:12; Habakkuk 3:2; Zechariah 8; Acts 3:19–20. I suggest you take time to search God's Word for ways to do revival praying through His Word. Ask the Lord to show you pictures of revival—maybe just a verse you can begin to use in your own life. [Also see the essay "Revival Praying from Psalm 107" (p. 53).]

A movement of prayer, however small, is essential for us to see revival. If we can gather even a small group to pray for revival, we may learn some day in heaven that the group was the "tipping point" God used to determine, "They're ready!" Revival is in His hands; He is the One who stirs us to prayer. God looks upon His people and says, "Oh, how desperately they need Me! I will start stirring them up" and He begins to stir up His people. Those who are responsive to His Spirit begin to pray and to teach others. God keeps calling us back to Himself, calling us to humble ourselves before Him and prepare our hearts for the work that He wants to do.

I believe that the revival that is to come will prepare the bride of Christ for the Bridegroom. The Word speaks of the bride being prepared, dressed in white, spotless, without blame. I believe what God is doing today is a process of preparing our hearts for a move of His Spirit, and part of that move is to bring in all who are coming. We live in significant times!

REVIVAL PRAYING FROM PSALM 107

Holy Scripture is filled with examples of the way that the people of God throughout the ages cried out to Him for revival. As we seek to pray effectively for revival in our land, we can use scriptural examples in praying for a move of God.

Psalm 107 is one of the clearest and most powerful pictures of revival praying in Scripture. Four times in this psalm, the people of God find themselves in dire straits and desperately seek God's intervention. As they pray, God's response is recorded and His presence and power are made manifest to His people.

It is really all about Jesus. Psalm 107 begins and ends with the Lord. In between, the psalmist marks the way the Lord steps into the lives of His people when they get serious about calling on His Name. Use this as a prayer guide as you learn to pray revival prayers.

Begin with Worship

We begin, as always, with worship. "Give thanks to the LORD, for He is good; his love endures forever. Let the redeemed of the LORD say this…" (vv. 1–2). Because we have time and again experienced the Lord's love and goodness, we launch our prayer with worship and thanksgiving.

Cry Out to the Lord

The heart of this prayer centers around four groups of people who are in dire straits. Though the primary group, of course, refers to the people of Israel, the psalm most certainly can be applied to the people of God down through the ages. The key to God's response in each case was the crying out by God's people. If we want to see God move in our midst, there must be a serious crying out of the church. I'm glad it says "cried out" instead of "prayed." We've watered down prayer to make it what we want, rather than what God wants.

The Wanderers

The first group of people in trouble is described in verses 4–5 as those who "wandered in desert wastelands, finding no way to a city where they could settle. They were hungry and thirsty, and their lives ebbed away." What a picture of the church today! In so many ways we are without direction and guidance, desperately needing even the basics (food and water) of our spiritual life. Hungry for God's presence (a city), we wander in dry places.

As we pray for the church and our own relationship to God, we need to ask Him for the wisdom He promises (James 1:5). We need wisdom for direction and guidance, trusting the Holy Spirit to bring us out of the dry places into the city promised to us, where the presence of God provides sustenance for all of life. "Then they cried out to the LORD in their trouble, and he delivered them from their distress. He led them by a straight way to a city where they could settle" (Psalm 107:6–7).

The Rebellious

The second group's story is found in verses 10–12: "Some sat in darkness and deepest gloom, prisoners suffering in iron chains, for they had rebelled against the words of God and despised the counsel of the Most High. So He subjected them to bitter labor; they stumbled, and there was no one to help."

Submission to the Word of God always results in a life of greater effectiveness in the kingdom and joy in the presence of the Lord. The believers in this passage discovered to their dismay that the opposite is true as well. Their rebellion against what God had said brought them to a point where they were literally in bondage. The practical result in their lives was bitter labor, which is work with no results. It is ineffective. How many of us have felt that way about our service to God? We work, we serve, but to what end? That is bitter labor.

What does it mean to rebel against God's Word? Certainly there are those who simply deny Scripture. That's an obvious means of rebellion. But most of those who read this essay firmly believe in the authority of the Bible. I want to suggest strongly that many of us who fervently believe God's Word are often still walking in rebellion because we hear the Word, but do not do it. James warns us about this type of rebellion: "Do not merely listen to the word, and so deceive yourselves. Do what it says" (James 1:22). Such rebellion is rampant in the church today. We have Bible study after Bible study, and yet our lives are no different. My brothers and sisters, this must change. God Himself has subjected us to bitter labor, dooming us to fruitless ministry until we submit ourselves to Him in obedience to His Word.

As we pray this psalm, we must ask ourselves, "Is there something God is calling me to do that I'm ignoring? Is there something my congregation or my family needs to submit to regarding the Word?" Pray over this situation and offer yourselves back to the Lord in submission to His Word. "Then they cried to the Lord in their trouble, and he saved them from their distress. He brought them out of darkness and the deepest gloom and broke away their chains" (Psalm 107:13–14).

The Spiritually Ill

Group three has literally become ill because of their rebellion against the Lord. The psalmist says, "Some became fools through their rebellious ways and suffered affliction because of their iniquities. They loathed all food and drew near the gates of death" (vv. 17–18). Sin can have fearful consequences in our lives, even as believers. Because these people continued in rebellion without repentance, God allowed them to "suffer affliction because of their iniquities."

If we are experiencing physical or spiritual illness because of our sin, the Bible is quick to show us the way for healing. Confession and healing are always paired together in God's plan. "There-fore confess your sins to each other and pray for each other so that you may be healed" (James 5:16). In 2 Chronicles 7:14, the heal-ing of the land is promised after there is a humbling of the people before God and a turning from sin. Confession always agrees with

God concerning the nature of sin and implies a turning from the commission of sin.

If we look to the body of Christ today and see spiritual and physical illness as a consequence of our rebellion, it is time to confess our sin. Would you take some quiet time before the Lord and ask Him what sins He sees in your or in the life of the church today? On behalf of the church, quickly confess all that you hear before Him as sin. Plead the blood of Jesus Christ over the sins of the church so that we might be healed: "Then they cried to the LORD in their trouble, and he saved them from their distress. He sent forth his word and healed them; he rescued them from the grave" (Psalm 107:19–20).

The Fearful

The last group is a bit different from the others, but, dear reader, you might find yourself right in the midst of these saints. These servants of the Lord are described as seafarers who "saw the works of the LORD, his wonderful deeds in the deep" (v. 24). But as storms arose, they became fearful. In verses 26–27 we read, "In their peril their courage melted away. They reeled and staggered like drunken men; they were at their wits' end."

Are you afraid as you consider the world around you and what seems to be a rise of wickedness? There is a real tendency for Christians to hide behind church walls, or in our fellowships, fearful of what may await us if we continue to serve the Lord. Many today face a spirit of timidity . . . a passive spirit that has given up on any hope of revival in the church. We sit and wait for the rapture to take us away, as though the Lord was done with His work on this planet.

It is time for the church to rise up! We must encounter this spirit of passivity head on with the courage that God gives us. God's word to Joshua as he led Israel into the Promised Land was "Be strong and courageous." We need to pray those words over one another today. "Then they cried out to the LORD in their trouble, and he brought them out of their distress. He stilled the storm to a whisper; the waves of the sea were hushed. They were glad when it grew calm, and he guided them to their desired haven" (Psalm 107:28–30). To strengthen us, let us allow these words of Jesus to flow into our prayer lives: "Take heart! I have overcome the world" (John 16:33).

We find ourselves in the midst of great trouble and turmoil as the people of God today. The solution is as clear for us as it was for these Old Testament saints: We must cry out to God! The revival of the church is awaiting those who will give themselves to God in serious intercession for His bride.

THE RESULT OF REVIVAL PRAYER

*M*any Christians are praying for revival without understanding what the end result might be if their prayers are truly answered. What might revival look like? We sometimes look to revivals in the past to catch a glimpse; however, the great revivals of history demonstrated unique characteristics that were often determined by the culture of their day. What God does in the future might look completely different.

There is a place, however, where we might find unchanging principles that will characterize revivals of both the past and the future. God's Word speaks much of revival and spiritual awakening. Sometimes the Bible tells of the difficult situations that prompt God's people to cry out for revival. At other times, Scripture helps us understand the type of praying and passion that prepares the way for a fresh move of God. In Isaiah 35, the entire chapter gives us a wonderful picture of the hope toward which we are praying.

As you read the text of Isaiah 35 below, please ask the Lord to point out to you these characteristics of revival: new life, the presence of God, strength, healing, outpouring of the Spirit, a lifestyle marked by holiness, and resulting joy.

The desert and the parched land will be glad; the wilderness will rejoice and blossom. Like the crocus, it will burst into bloom; it will rejoice greatly and shout for joy. The glory of Lebanon will be given to it, the splendor of Carmel and Sharon; they will see the glory of the LORD, the splendor of our God.

Strengthen the feeble hands, steady the knees that give way; say to those with fearful hearts, "Be strong, do not fear; your God will come, he will come with vengeance; with divine retribution he will come to save you."

Then will the eyes of the blind be opened and the ears of the deaf unstopped. Then will the lame leap like a deer, and the mute tongue shout for joy. Water will gush forth in the wilderness and streams in the desert. The burning sand will become a pool, the thirsty ground bubbling springs. In the haunts where jackals once lay, grass and reeds and papyrus will grow.

And a highway will be there; it will be called the Way of Holiness. The unclean will not journey on it; it will be for those who walk in that Way; wicked fools will not go about on it. No lion will be there, nor will any ferocious beast get up on it; they will not be found there. But only the redeemed will walk there, and the ransomed of the LORD will return. They will enter Zion with singing; everlasting joy will crown their heads. Gladness and joy will overtake them, and sorrow and sighing will flee away.

One of the first signs of revival is new life. Whether it is an individual or a church, when revival begins, there is evidence of life and growth. The very word "revive" means to bring back to life. Isaiah draws a picture of a dry desert that appears to be lacking in life. But when it begins to rain, the buried seed bursts into the glorious color of life.

This new life is marked by a fresh vision of God: "They will see the glory of the LORD, the splendor of our God." What previous writers have often called, "the manifest presence of God" is spoken of here. The presence of God's Spirit in the life of a believer is a biblical fact. The great need for revival, however, is indicated by the failure of most believers to walk in an awareness of His presence. In times of revival, God's presence is manifested in such a way that believers are often overwhelmed by the experience.

Renewed strength is often an indicator that God is moving in a new way in our life. The natural tendency is to wear down and burn out in service and ministry. The fresh awareness of Christ working within us through His Spirit often calls forth new levels of energy and productivity among kingdom workers.

The outpouring of God's precious Holy Spirit is many times accompanied by physical healing. The deep work of God within the spirit of an individual often spills over to touch the body as well. Isaiah speaks of the blind, deaf, lame, and mute experiencing a healing touch from the Lord. What will happen universally for the people of God in eternity happens in the Lord's timing and choosing in the midst of revival.

Water is often a symbol for the Holy Spirit. In the seventh chapter of the Gospel of John, Jesus poured out water in Jerusalem on the greatest day of the Feast of Tabernacles. The apostle John interpreted this accurately for us by saying that Jesus was speaking of the Holy Spirit who would become a gushing stream coming forth from within us (John 7:38-39). In this, he echoes the imagery of Isaiah, who described water gushing forth in the wilderness . . . a dry place, and streams in the midst of the wilderness.

When we pray for revival, one of the clearest results will be an outpouring of the Holy Spirit upon believers. Life-giving, pure, renewing water flows from the lives of Christians, attracting others who find themselves strangely thirsty in the midst of this spiritual abundance.

Revival always produces a change in lifestyle. We ought to view with suspicion any supposed move of God that does not result in a life of increased holiness. If the Spirit of holiness has been poured out in fresh waves, we will see a new passion to live lives that please the Lord in every way.

It will not surprise us to see that overwhelming joy is one of the most visible marks of revival. What other response could there be for the believer who has suddenly been made aware of the loving presence of Christ in a fresh new way? As we experience His life, the fullness of His Spirit produces joy that absolutely overwhelms any tendency toward sighing or crying. Isaiah's description of "everlasting joy" crowning our heads places this joy in a prominent place in our lives where all can see what God has done.

What are you expecting to see when revival comes? Let the prophet Isaiah keep you focused on what God desires to happen in the midst of this next great awakening. May this great vision of a holy, healed, strong, and joyful people keep you praying fervently for revival in our day!

JOSIAH'S REVIVAL

One of the greatest recorded revivals took place in the southern kingdom of Judah during the reign of Josiah. As we pray and long for revival today, looking back at this biblical revival can help us understand more of what it is we are seeking. This account is found in chapters 34 and 35 of 2 Chronicles.

Josiah was just eight years old when he became king. As a teenager, something happened that caused him to begin to seek after the Lord. Second Chronicles 34:3 says, "In the eighth year of his reign, while he was still young, he began to seek the God of his father David." This sixteen-year-old king began to develop a hunger to know God. At an age when, at least today, we expect little in the way of spiritual depth, God was stirring in the heart of this young man. Many of us who are longing for revival today believe that it will be birthed in the hearts and lives of the younger generations among us. Josiah is a good model of such a youth-driven revival.

Like his ancestor David, young Josiah had learned to focus his desire on that which was truly important. It was God Himself that Josiah sought. It is God alone who truly satisfies and who, in Himself, is the only reasonable desire of His people. You will never find yourself longing for revival until you first find yourself desiring God Himself.

Perhaps the question that all of us must ask is this: "What are we truly seeking in our lives at this moment?" What is it that drives us, motivates us, and gives us a reason to get up in the morning? As Christians, we can still find ourselves with an inadequate apologetic for our lives. We may have a Christian veneer, but inside, we may be seeking the same things as our nonreligious neighbors. Does success drive us? Is it money or security that we are seeking? Perhaps it is happiness, personal peace, or a good family that becomes our desire.

Josiah acted upon his seeking heart when he began a process of repentance and turning from sin that impacted him personally, as well as the entire nation of Judah. In verses 3–7 of 2 Chronicles 34, we see that Josiah led the nation in purging the land of its idols. In all true revival, there must be a turning from sin.

As the nation turned from idolatry, there became a natural turning toward God. The young king ordered his servants to begin to repair the abandoned temple, the place of worship for Judah. As the temple was cleaned and repaired, it was also restored as a place of worship. True worship will always be a mark of genuine revival. As the presence of the Lord is experienced by His people, worship will be the natural response of those whose hearts are set on God.

Verses 14–19 tell of an exciting discovery that was made. As the temple was being repaired, the workmen discovered the lost scrolls of the Law. Judah had fallen away so completely from God that they had literally lost God's Word. The rediscovery of the Word set the nation up to be blessed and to experience the presence of God in a powerful way.

The rediscovery of God's Word is needed in our own culture today. In many lives, the Word has been lost. It has been unopened and unread. In many cases, even when it is read, it has not been revered, respected, believed, or obeyed. One of the key marks of a genuine revival from God is the restoration of the authority of the Bible.

What happened next in the story of Josiah is so important for the church today to comprehend. When the Law was found, the king had a heart that was responsive to what God had said. Josiah led the nation in repentance over its failure to obey the Word. With that repentance came a recommitment to not merely read it, but to act upon it. With Josiah leading the way, the nation now put itself under the authority of the Word of God.

The role of leadership cannot be overstated here. As you read the following passage of Scripture, note that it was clearly the king who held the people accountable:

> Then the king called together all the elders of Judah and Jerusalem. He went up to the temple of the LORD with the men of Judah, the people of Jerusalem, the priests and the Levites—all the people from the least to the greatest. He read in their hearing all the words of the Book of the Covenant, which had been found in the temple of the LORD. The king stood by his pillar and renewed the covenant in the presence of the LORD—to follow the LORD and keep his commands, regulations and decrees with all his heart and all his soul, and to obey the words of the covenant written in this book. Then he had everyone in Jerusalem and Benjamin pledge themselves to it; the people of Jerusalem did this in accordance with the covenant of God, the God of their fathers. (2 Chronicles 34:29–32)

What a wonderful picture of the need for the church today to respond to the authority of the Bible. It is not merely in reading or hearing the Word that we are changed. We are to be doers of the Word. God calls us to listen and obey. Revival breaks out where there is a radical obedience to the Bible.

We cannot finish looking at Josiah's revival without seeing the excitement brought about by a new awareness of the Lord's presence with His people. The first nineteen verses of Second Chronicles 35 deal with an awesome time of celebration during which Judah observed the greatest Passover feast in Israel's history. Verse 18 says, "The Passover had not been observed like this in Israel since the days of the prophet Samuel; and none of the kings of Israel had ever celebrated such a Passover as did Josiah . . ."

Great rejoicing is the result of returning to the Lord and experiencing His reviving power. It is important for the church today to notice that it was not celebration that ushered in revival, but repentance and radical obedience to the Word of God. Celebration was the result of God's acceptance and forgiveness.

As the church continues to long for and to pray for revival, we would do well to look to this young man Josiah and his amazing leadership over the nation of Judah. May the Lord raise up many young men and women like Josiah who will earnestly seek the Lord, and in doing so, lead us into a still greater experience of the presence of Christ!

THE ROLE OF PRAYER IN REVIVAL

The following is edited from a message given at the Heart-Cry for Revival Conference in November 2009 at The Cove, Asheville, North Carolina, U.S.A. Used by permission.

When it comes to the issue of revival, prayer is ultimately where it begins and continues. We cannot make revival happen, but we can ask for it. Most people believe that prayer must take place before God moves.

Many authors down through the years have agreed. Martyn Lloyd-Jones said, "The main reason we should be praying about revival is that we are anxious to see God's name vindicated and His glory manifested. We should be anxious to see something happening that will arrest the nations, all the peoples, and cause them to stop and think again."

C. H. Spurgeon wrote this: "Oh! men and brethren, what would this heart feel if I could but believe that there were some among you who would go home and pray for a revival—men whose faith is large enough, and their love fiery enough to lead them from this moment to exercise unceasing intercessions that God would appear among us and do wondrous things here as in the times of former generations."

John R. Mott said, "If added power attends united prayer of two or three, what mighty triumphs there will be when hundreds of thousands of consistent members of the church are, with one accord, day by day, making intercession for the extension of Christ's kingdom."

We could produce by the thousands, quotations of men and women of God throughout the years who have understood the role of prayer in a great move of God. If we are to see God move in our day, then it will be because at least some will have given themselves to asking Him to fulfill the desire of His heart to awaken His people.

A Time of Revival in Judah

Second Chronicles chapters 14 through 20 tells of a time of revival in Judah. These chapters are basically the story of sixty-five years in the life of the nation of Judah in which there were seasons of revival. During these years, Asa and his son Jehoshaphat were seeking God and doing some things that God used to bring awakening to Judah.

Judah desperately needed awakening. After the death of Solomon, the kingdom had divided into the southern kingdom (Judah) and the northern kingdom (Israel). Rehoboam, Solomon's son, was king of Judah. Jeroboam and others went into the northern kingdom of Israel. For the rest of the history of Israel, there were no godly kings. But through the history of Judah, again and again God would raise up a godly king who would draw Judah, the people of God, back to Himself. After Rehoboam died, the next king of Judah was his son Abijah, who was ungodly. But when Abijah's son, Asa, became king, he was committed to following God: "Asa did what was good and right in the eyes of the LORD his God. He removed the foreign altars and the high places, smashed the sacred stones and cut down the Asherah poles. He commanded Judah to seek the LORD, the God of their fathers...." (2 Chronicles 14:2–4). Asa had ten long years of peace and devoted his energy to turning Judah back to God.

Then, ten years into his reign, there came a sudden invasion, and Asa prayed a godly prayer that God used to bring victory to the people of God. About five years later, there came a time of great celebration. Revival literally broke out among the people of God as they sought Him with all their hearts. They offered great sacrifices to Him. It was a time of great rejoicing.

This lasted for a number of years in the life of Judah. Asa did not end well, however, and the revival ended in the last years of his life. A crisis had developed in the nation as Israel to the north gathered forces to attack Judah. This time, instead of depending on the Lord in faith as Asa had done earlier, he used some of the temple treasury to bribe a pagan king to attack Israel to keep them from coming against Judah. It ended in victory for Judah, but it was not the way God wanted them to gain the victory. The Lord's prophet came and rebuked Asa, but Asa did not receive it well, and he threw the prophet into jail.

During the rest of his life, Asa did not seek God fully. At one point he had a severe disease in his feet, yet even then he did not seek the Lord. Asa died with a shadow over the end of his life.

But his son Jehoshaphat picked up the best characteristics of his father and became one of the greatest kings of Judah. His heart was fully set on the Lord. He, too, worked hard at removing all the remaining idols from the land. The Scripture says that the nations around Jehoshaphat gave them peace on every side, and a fear of God was on the other nations because they saw that God was with Jehoshaphat. Jehoshaphat did something amazing. He commissioned and trained others to go among the people and teach the Word of God. There is even suggestion in Scripture that King Jehoshaphat himself went out and began to teach others the Word of God, and he commanded them to seek the Lord their God.

Then there came—once again—a great battle, when an alliance of three kings came against Jehoshaphat. Most of Judah had to hide behind the walls of Jerusalem. Jehoshaphat led his people in a time of prayer that released the power of God and caused one of the most amazing victories that Judah ever saw. Once again, revival broke out among the people of God.

Off and on for sixty-five years, God moved in the life of His people. There are two prayers in these chapters of 2 Chronicles that can be models for us. One is from Asa, the other from Jehoshaphat. What you see in Asa and Jehoshaphat is that prayer preceded revival, prayer pervaded revival (it was all through the midst of it), and prayer propelled revival (expanded it, took it to new places). What happened in their lives can happen in ours!

Prayer Principles from Asa's Prayer

Asa's prayer is found in 2 Chronicles 14:11. There are principles for praying for revival found in this prayer. Beginning in verse 9, the situation is described: "Zerah the Cushite marched out against them with a vast army and three hundred chariots, and came as far as Mareshah. Asa went out to meet him, and they took up battle positions in the Valley of Zephathah near Mareshah. Then Asa called to the LORD his God and said, 'LORD, there is no one like you to help the powerless against the mighty. Help us, O LORD our God, for we rely on you, and in your name we have come against this vast army. O LORD, You are our God; do not let man prevail against you'" (vv. 9–11).

The first principle is that Asa humbled himself before God. He called upon God "to help the powerless against the mighty." Who were the powerless in this situation? Asa and Judah. There was a much mightier army coming against them. The king of Judah was standing in front of his people with his army behind him, and he humbled himself in the sight of all the people. He said in effect, "God, You are the powerful One. You are the One who hears prayers and we are coming as the powerless to You. We desperately need Your help!"

As we pray for revival, one of the great needs is the prayer of humility. Asa humbled himself and made a simple request: "Help us." He did not try to tell God what to do. Sometimes our prayers simply need to be, "God, revive us!" This is what we need.

When Asa prayed for the Lord's help, he prayed for the right reasons. He was concerned for the Lord's honor and not simply the preservation of his life and the life of his people. At the end of this prayer, he prayed, "LORD our God . . . we rely on you, and in your name we have come against this vast army. O LORD, you are our God; do not let man prevail against you." The reason he asked for help was ultimately for the honor and glory of God. Notice he said, "Do not let man prevail against you."

We need to understand that most of the people of Asa's day had a tribal deity, a god. These gods were demons masquerading as gods, but nonetheless, the tribes all identified with a particular god. There was always the idea that if our god is stronger than your god, then we will win. Earlier in Israel's history, because of their sin, Israel was conquered by the Philistines and the ark of the covenant was captured. The Philistines took the ark of the covenant into the temple of their god, Dagon, because they thought the god Dagon had defeated the God of Israel. In their minds, their god was now greater. Of course, it was dismaying to them the next morning when they found that Dagon had fallen before Jehovah and the ark of the covenant. (See I Samuel 5:1–4.)

In the context of the pagan world around him, Asa prayed something like this: "O God, they are coming against us and they are much mightier and more powerful than we are, and we cannot begin to beat them. God, do not let them beat You! Do not let their god receive glory when You are the One that needs to receive the glory!" When we are praying for revival, the purpose is ultimately about Christ and His glory, about His receiving honor.

Prayer Principles from Jehoshaphat's Prayer

In 2 Chronicles 20, we see Asa's son Jehoshaphat praying correctly in a time of crisis. Three nations had allied together to come and destroy Judah. Here is how Jehoshaphat prayed as he stood in front of the assembly of all the people:

> O LORD, God of our fathers, are you not the God who is in heaven? You rule over all the kingdoms of the nations. Power and might are in your hand, and no one can withstand you. O our God, did you not drive out the inhabitants of this land before your people Israel and give it

forever to the descendants of Abraham your friend? They have lived in it and have built in it a sanctuary for your Name, saying, "If calamity comes upon us, whether the sword of judgment, or plague or famine, we will stand in your presence before this temple that bears your Name and will cry out to you in our distress, and you will hear us and save us."

But now here are men from Ammon, Moab and Mount Seir, whose territory you would not allow Israel to invade when they came from Egypt; so they turned away from them and did not destroy them. See how they are repaying us by coming to drive us out of the possession you gave us as an inheritance. O our God, will you not judge them? For we have no power to face this vast army that is attacking us. We do not know what to do, but our eyes are upon you. (2 Chronicles 20:6-12)

Jehoshaphat affirmed the Lord's power over the nations. Even though he saw that, from a human perspective, Judah was much weaker and had no ability to handle what was coming at them, the prayer began by saying in effect, "God, You are over the nations. They do not know it, but You are in charge of them." I think today as we look at what is going on around us there are times for us to say, "Lord, the evil ruler of _____ does not know it, but You are in charge. The president of _____ does not know it, but You are in charge. That terrorist organization does not understand Your position, but You rule the nations." It is important for us to have that proper perspective as we come in prayer. Sometimes these nations, these situations look to be so big, so huge. Jehoshaphat prayed with this correct understanding of who God is and how He relates to the nations.

Then he affirms Judah's right to pray. He goes back and quotes his great-great-grandfather Solomon who, as he was dedicating the temple, spoke to God, saying that when they find themselves in times of trouble, they are going to come here to the temple and are going to pray to ask Him to intervene. God spoke to Solomon and said, "If my people, who are called by my name, will humble themselves and pray and seek my face and turn from their wicked ways, then will I hear from heaven and will forgive their sin and will heal their land" (2 Chronicles 7:14).

So Jehoshaphat based his prayer not just on what he wanted but on what God's Word said. This is how we pray with boldness and effectiveness—we learn to pray the Word of God. That is where the power is in prayer. It is no longer us trying to talk God into giving us something we want, but it is coming to God who has already placed within our hearts what He desires to happen. We begin to pray His heart, His agenda, His will.

This kind of prayer is also a prayer of humility. Jehoshaphat calls out to God, "We have no power to face this vast army…. We do not know what to do, but our eyes are upon you" (2 Chronicles 20:12). One thing that makes this prayer so amazing is who prayed it. This is a king in a time of crisis, praying this prayer not in the privacy of his own chambers, but in front of all the people. This situation was not so different than what we face today. We want our leaders to know the answers. A nation wants someone to lead. Jehoshaphat performs this act of humility where the leader of the people stands up and prays something like this: "God, I do not know what to do. Here is what I do know: I am going to keep my eyes fixed on You."

Imagine what would happen in a nation if the president stood up and said, "The crises around us are great. I have been praying and I have been reading Scripture, and I have to tell you, I do not know what to do. But here is what I am going to do: I am going to keep my eyes fixed on the Lord." We need to pray for those in leadership that God would grip their hearts and that they would begin to pray like Jehoshaphat when faced with these kinds of crises.

Prayer Precedes Revival

In each of these cases, prayer preceded revival. Before God poured out His Spirit, before everything took place, prayer took place. You can see that same thing in all revivals down through history. There was a movement of prayer in anticipation of the work of God.

What kinds of prayers precede revival? There may be others, but there are two kinds of prayers that take place, that need to happen right now. First is the prayer of *repentance.* In 2 Chronicles 14 when Asa commanded Judah to seek the Lord, immediately they began to tear down all of the foreign altars. Those are acts of repentance, acts based on their prayers in which they sought the Lord and they realized they could not seek the Lord and have idols. We need to focus more of our teaching on repentance.

Second is the prayer of *desperation.* Jehoshaphat, in a sense, prayed that kind of prayer: "God, I have no Plan B. There is only Plan A, and it is whatever You are going to do. We are desperate, Lord, for You to move." In the life of the church today in America, we have not yet come to the point of desperation. We still have plans and programs; we are still going to this conference and that conference, trying to find the right sort of thing that will get our people going again. We have not yet reached a place of desperation. Prayers of repentance and desperation are the sort of prayers that precede revival.

As I travel, I do not find many praying churches. There are frustrated pastors and prayer leaders who would love for their churches to become praying churches, but there is not much going on. They get discouraged when they have a prayer meeting and just a handful of people come. But God has a remnant He is working through. Weary people need to stick with it, and they need not give up. God is looking for this remnant to humble themselves before God. As they do, they will continue to grow and build and develop. That is what God is looking for to spark revival. Then there will come a day when our prayer meetings will be full. People will come to prayer meetings because that is where they experience the presence of Christ in a fresh, new way.

Prayer Pervades Revival

When revival begins, prayer does not end. In fact, when prayer ends, the revival ends. One of the marks of revival is continued prayer, day and night prayer. Whole cities become like prayer meetings as people pray on the street corners. What kind of prayer pervades revival? It is a prayer of *humility*—a prayer like Asa prayed in 2 Chronicles 14:11: "O God, help us!" That kind of prayer of humility is what will continue revival, because one of the things that will stop revival is pride. If suddenly our churches are filled, if suddenly things are moving, then there is a tendency for us to begin to take credit, to feel like we have accomplished something. To continue to have prayer pervade revival, we must be praying prayers of humility, recognizing that what we have comes from God, that it is not by our own effort, but it is what He has done.

I believe also that the prayers of *worship* and *thankfulness* are needed. These are two different things, but I bring them together because you see them together in the lives of Asa and Jehoshaphat: (1) prayers of *worship*, adoring God, recognizing Him for who He is; and (2) prayers of *thankfulness*, of gratitude. Jehoshaphat and his people fell down and worshiped God in 2 Chronicles 20:18, and then some Levites felt led to stand up and praise God in verse 19. Praise and singing continued even as the army marched out. In fact, praise was so important that a group of singers was dispatched *ahead* of the army. Prayer pervades revival.

Prayer Propels Revival

Prayer propels revival. It expands it, takes it to new places. Biblically and historically, when revival took place, it went outward and spread to other places. The people of God experiencing the presence of God could not contain it. They began to pray different sorts of prayers, prayers that took the revival to different places. They began to pray evangelistic and transformational types of prayers. Jehoshaphat is a great example of one whose "heart was devoted to the ways of the LORD" (2 Chronicles 17:6). But then he took what God was doing in his life out to the nation. He himself, as well as others that he trained, took the Word of God and went to the people to teach them to seek the Lord and to obey the Lord in all ways. Prayers of transformation and evangelism, lifestyle-type praying is the sort of thing I believe that God is calling the church to when revival takes place, and it is to be expanded and propelled in other places. The Holy Spirit is the spark that ignites revival and causes it to be propelled.

In Heaven's Throne Room

I want to invite you into the throne room. In Hebrews 4:16, the writer commands us, "Let us then approach the throne of grace with confidence, so that we may receive mercy and find grace to help us in our time of need." The Bible teaches us that somehow when we turn our thoughts toward heaven, when we begin to pray in a way beyond our comprehension, then we come into the throne room of heaven. Have you ever thought about that, about what really happens when you pray? The Bible says that we go to the throne room. Have you thought about the throne room?

John, in the Book of Revelation, has difficulty describing the magnificence of the throne room. There is the great white throne of the Father on the sea like glass, then to His right hand is the throne of Jesus Christ, His Son, and around the throne of the Father and the Son are four living creatures whose sole task is to cry out for all eternity, "Holy, holy, holy is the Lord God Almighty..." (4:8). Around those four are twenty-four elders with crowns of gold. They are on their own thrones, and they are continually taking their crowns and casting them at the feet of Jesus and worshiping Him. And if that were not enough, the Bible tells us that the throne room of heaven is filled with a myriad of angels who are gathered together in joyful assembly. (See Revelation 4–5.)

I always picture a little door at the back of the great throne room. When we begin to pray, I picture that the door opens and we walk in right down the center of the throne room, right up to the throne of grace. And if we begin to pray short and fast and then we turn to leave, I imagine the angels saying, "That's it? That's all he is going to ask for? He had the attention of the eternal Father, and he muttered a few phrases and left?"

God is calling us to the throne room. We are even now seated with Christ in the heavenly places (Eph. 2:6). This is where we belong. And in the throne room come all these other scenes that you see in the Book of Revelation of the glory of the Lamb of God who is also the Lion. We begin to catch a glimpse of the passionate heart of God for the rule of Christ over all the earth. He is waiting on us to ask Him to do what He wants to do on planet Earth today. Come to the throne room! Together, let us pray:

> Father, surrounded by Your glory and majesty, comforted by Your grace and love, we bow before You and worship You. Forgive us of our prayerlessness, for thinking that somehow by our words and our wisdom we can do it. As we humble ourselves before You, help us to stay in Your presence. Teach us to pray according to Your will and purpose so that Christ will be exalted in the midst of Your people. Teach us to pray in a way that releases Your power, that we might see Your purpose accomplished to the ends of the earth. In Jesus' name we pray. Amen.

If you would like to read more essays by Dave Butts, visit www. harvestprayer.com.

Let It Begin In Me

ONE1CRY

A Nationwide Call for Spiritual Awakening

TURN // PRAY // UNITE

in humble repentance from every sin God reveals to us

with urgency for spiritual recovery and awakening

with other believers in spreading the hope of revival

To learn more about OneCry and to join the movement, visit

www.onecry.com